FIGHTING TO SURVIVE IN THE WILDERNESS
TERRIFYING TRUE STORIES

By Eric Braun

COMPASS POINT BOOKS
a capstone imprint

Compass Point Books are published by Capstone Press
1710 Roe Crest Drive, North Mankato, Minnesota 56003
www.capstonepub.com

Library of Congress Cataloging-in-Publication Data
Names: Braun, Eric, 1971– author.
Title: Fighting to survive in the wilderness : terrifying true stories / by Eric Braun.
Description: North Mankato, Minnesota : Compass Point Books, an imprint of Capstone Press, [2020] | Series: Fighting to survive | Audience: Ages: 10 to 14. | Includes bibliographical references and index.
Identifiers: LCCN 2019005972| ISBN 9780756561871 (hardcover)
ISBN 9780756562342 (pbk.) ISBN 9780756562090 (eBook PDF)
Subjects: LCSH: Wilderness survival—Juvenile literature. | Disasters—Juvenile literature. | Disaster victims—Biography—Juvenile literature.
Classification: LCC GV200.5 .B73 2020 | DDC 613.6/9--dc23
LC record available at https://lccn.loc.gov/2019005972

Editorial Credits
Kristen Mohn, editor; Terri Poburka, designer; Morgan Walters, media researcher; Kathy McColley, production specialist

Photo Credits
Alamy: Angelo Andreas Zinna, 44, Cavan Images, 9, 13; Associated Press, 58; Associated Press: Jon Freilich, 47; Getty Images: John Peters, 17, Thierry Falise, 18; iStockphoto: DanielPrudek, 42; Newscom: CAPT. JESSICA TAIT/UPI, 21, GARY CASKEY/REUTERS, 15, Polaris, 23, 25, Thai Navy SEALs/ZUMA Press, 26; Shutterstock: Anton Rogozin, 39, Artemfil, 35, Det.Sherlock, 54, f11photo, 7, Featureflash Photo Agency, 49, Isaac Marzioli, (ink) design element throughout, Kristina Ponomareva, (trees) Cover, Miloje, (paper) design element, Paolo Cremonesi, (hands) Cover, Rainer Lesniewski, 51, rickyd, 5, RPBaiao, 57, xpixel, (grunge) design element throughout; The Image Works: TopFoto, 29, 33, 37; Wikimedia: Library of Congress, top 31, NormanEinstein, bottom 31, RuthAS, 52-53

Printed and bound in the USA.
PA71

TABLE OF
CONTENTS

INTRODUCTION **4**

AFTER THE END OF THE WORLD
Aron Ralston.. **6**

**IN THE MOUNTAIN OF
THE SLEEPING LADY**
The Wild Boars Soccer Team.............................. **16**

ALONE AGAINST THE ARCTIC
Ada Blackjack.. **28**

A NIGHT IN THE DEATH ZONE
Beck Weathers... **38**

DROPPED INTO THE AMAZON
Juliane Koepcke.. **50**

Glossary **60**
Read More **61**
Internet Sites **61**
Source Notes **62**
Select Bibliography **63**
Index.. **64**

INTRODUCTION

People are heading outside to hike and camp in record numbers. State and national parks are seeing a surge in visitors. In 2017 the National Park Service had more than 330 million visitors. The great outdoors attracts us for the scenery, the solitude, and chance to experience adventure in an untamed world.

But as more people get out, more people also get lost or hurt. In 2016 rangers in the Adirondack Mountains of New York were forced to go on an average of one search-and-rescue operation per day. That's in part because amateur explorers sometimes show up unprepared for the adventure that attracted them. They don't bring water, food, proper clothing, maps, matches, or other essential survival items. If something bad happens, they can quickly find themselves in big trouble.

Even seasoned adventurers can make mistakes. Some of the people discussed in this book were experienced climbers and hikers. Aron Ralston had hiked several 14,000-foot (4,267-meter) mountains and explored many canyons and desert landscapes. But he made the near-fatal mistake of not telling anyone where he was going. The Wild Boars soccer team had explored the caves around their home before. But they made the mistake of going deep into a cave before seasonal rains flooded it.

For others, there was no way to prepare for what happened to them. The ship that was supposed to bring supplies for Ada Blackjack and her companions never showed up. Juliane Koepcke's airplane crashed in a remote rain forest. Good planning couldn't compensate for that.

What everyone discussed in this book does have in common is that they survived. They found themselves in dire situations, but they didn't give up. They faced off against death, and death backed down.

AFTER THE END OF THE WORLD
ARON RALSTON

Aron Ralston finally got mad—so mad that he began thrashing back and forth in the narrow canyon. In a furious rage, he screamed and banged his body against the stone walls. His anguished voice echoed up the canyon.

The frustration had finally boiled over. Trapped alone in a desert crevasse for more than five days, he had remained disciplined and calm—remarkable considering that his arm was smashed beneath a boulder, pinning him where he was. He had carefully meted out his precious supply of food and water. He had considered the options of how to free himself. And he had gathered up the courage to carry out his only option to survive.

A LIFE OF ADVENTURE

The 27-year-old hiker should never have been in this position. Ralston was an experienced hiker, rock climber, biker, and skier. Born in Ohio, he and his family moved to Denver, Colorado, when he was 11 years old. There, he fell in love with outdoor adventures. He liked to be alone in nature. He was also a good student. In college he earned degrees in mechanical engineering and French. After a stint in Arizona as a mechanical engineer, he returned to Colorado and life in the mountains.

Ralston set a goal to climb all of Colorado's "fourteeners," mountains with peaks higher than 14,000 feet (4,267 m). He wanted to be the first person to accomplish this challenge alone in the winter. But by the spring of 2003, he hadn't achieved his goal. With winter over, he turned his focus to other hikes. He would pick up his fourteener challenge the following winter.

On Saturday, April 26, Ralston set out for the tiny Utah town of Moab, nicknamed the "end of the world." When he reached Moab, he kept on driving. Two and a half hours later, he arrived at the trailhead for Horseshoe Canyon. Nearly five hours away from home, well past the "end of the world," he was just where he wanted to be—alone at the beginning of an adventure.

Ralston was hiking in Canyonlands, Utah's largest national park, covering nearly 340,000 acres (1,376 square kilometers).

As an experienced hiker, Ralston had prepared well for his day. He had packed his hiking boots, backpack, climbing equipment, and a hydration system. He had two burritos and a few chunks of chocolate. He'd also packed a pocket-sized utility knife and a video camera. He even brought his mountain bike to ride into the desert before his hike.

He had thought of almost everything. What he hadn't brought was a cell phone. Even worse, he hadn't told anyone where he was going.

The red sand, rock formations, and caverns in this remote part of Utah are beautiful. Ralston biked through the stunning landscape. Eventually he locked his wheel to his frame and left the bike under a tree to begin his hike. He hiked for a while with two women he met, then left them to explore the Bluejohn Canyon. He was "canyoneering," exploring the canyon by free-climbing, climbing with ropes, and making daring jumps across deep, narrow openings. It's difficult terrain that requires strong technical skills to navigate. Ralston was more than up to the task.

"I was accustomed to being in far, far riskier environments," he later said. "So I thought going into that canyon was a walk in the park—there were no avalanches, it was a beautiful day, and I was essentially just walking."

SLOW-MOTION SLIP

That changed when Ralston suddenly slipped while negotiating a 3-foot- (1-m-) wide gap over a 10-foot (3-m) drop. He slid and, in the process, dislodged a large boulder that had appeared to be secure.

Later he would remember the fall as happening in "slow motion." When he looked up, the 800-pound (360-kilogram)

Bluejohn Canyon, where Ralston
was trapped, is called a slot canyon
because it is very deep and narrow.

boulder crashed down and crushed his right hand against the side of the canyon, wedging it into place. For a second, he said, the situation seemed funny.

Then the pain hit. He screamed and cursed for several minutes, unable to get his hand out. He took a long drink from his water, bottle, but he quickly realized he had to make that water last. It was all he had, and he didn't know how long he'd be stuck. Ralston forced himself to calm down and think. Nobody knew where he was, so he couldn't hope for a rescue. If he wanted to get out alive, it was up to him.

His first idea was to move or break up the boulder. He shoved against it, but it wouldn't budge. He used his utility knife to try to chip it apart, but the big rock was too hard. All he was doing was dulling his blade. As the sun went down over the desert, he began to feel very alone. He thought briefly of suicide, but he ruled it out. He intended to survive, somehow.

Although he didn't want to admit it at first, the answer was obvious. He recalled thinking out loud about it. "There's this surreal conversation with myself. 'Aron, you're gonna have to cut your arm off!' 'I don't want to cut my arm off!' 'Dude, you're gonna have to cut your arm off.' I said it to myself. That little back-and-forth."

DID YOU KNOW?

Actor James Franco starred in a 2010 movie, *127 Hours,* about Ralston's ordeal. Ralston said the movie was very faithful to his real experience.

A BIG DECISION

The next day Ralston kept trying to break up the rock with his knife, but it was no use. He devised a system with his climbing ropes and pulleys to try to lift the boulder. But that, too, was useless. By now his hand was not looking very good. It hadn't gotten circulation in about two days, and the flesh was decaying. He cut into his thumb with the knife to see if he could feel anything. He could not. When he cut, a hissing sound came out. It was air from the decomposition.

Finally he resolved to cut off the dead limb. He opened the knife blade, put it against his arm, and began sawing. And sawing.

The blade was too dull to even break the skin.

Ralston folded up the blade and opened the tool's smaller blade. It was only 2 inches (5 centimeters) long, but it was sharper than the big blade. Instead of sawing, Ralston started the cut by stabbing into his arm.

He kept cutting, but when he reached bone, he realized that his knife was not strong enough to get through. Nothing he had could cut through the bone. It was hopeless. Moments ago he had resolved to do it. He had somehow found the courage to amputate his arm so he could free himself. Now his courage didn't matter, because he didn't have the means to do it. He believed he was going to die there.

Ralston set up his video camera in the cavern and recorded himself. He talked to his parents, and he gave his last will and testament. He begged anyone who found the camera to locate his parents and give them the video.

On the fifth night—exhausted, thirsty, hungry, cold, and in terrible pain—Ralston began to hallucinate. He saw a small boy. And he saw himself there, with only one hand, playing with the boy. It was a vision of himself in the future, he believed. He would one day have a son.

Now, Ralston was determined. *I am going to get through this night,* he thought.

A FLASH OF ANGER—AND HOPE

The next morning, as the desert sun cast
the cavern in deep shadow, Ralston became
angry. His plan—the only plan he had—was not
working. Despairing and desperate, he did what
most people would have done days earlier. He
threw a fit. He screamed and thrashed. In the
midst of his thrashing, he noticed something. His
arm did not budge, but it did bend . . . in a very
wrong way. Like it was about to break.

Suddenly his hope was renewed. "I felt my
bone bend and I realized I could use the boulder
to break it," he said later. "It was like fireworks
going off—I was going to get out of there."

So, steeling himself against the pain, he
used the weight of his body to bend his arm
against the boulder until the bone snapped. The
pain was terrible, but he picked up the knife with
its small blade and began cutting again.

"I had this huge grin on my face as I picked
up that knife to start this horrific thing," he said. "It was traumatic,
but it was a blessing to be able to get out of there."

Ralston cut through skin and muscle. The pain was intense,
like molten metal running up his arm and into his body, but he
remained focused. Knowing that he was working on a solution
helped him stay calm. After cutting for a while, he saw an artery.
It was only then that he realized he would be at risk of bleeding to
death. So, using the rubber line from his hydration pack, he twisted
a tourniquet on his upper arm. That would stop the bleeding after
the amputation.

The boulder that trapped Ralston's arm was estimated to weigh about 800 pounds (360 kg).

As Ralston cut through the artery, blood gushed out. The canyon wall was covered in blood. He kept going, cutting through more muscle and two more arteries. Then he reached a tendon, the hardest layer to cut. His knife blade couldn't do the job, so he took out the pliers tool, grasped the tendon, and wrenched until it tore through.

The pain was already searing, but what he saw next was going to be the most difficult part of all. A long, thin line ran along his arm like a piece of spaghetti. It was his nerve. Ralston slid the blade under it, and immediately that burning-liquid-metal sensation flared up. He yanked and snapped the nerve, and the pain doubled. But the hard part was over.

He continued sawing at what was left of his flesh until suddenly he fell backward onto the ground. He was free.

NEW LIFE

After creating a makeshift sling for his stump, Ralston stumbled out of the cavern. He described that moment as being reborn, because he had already accepted that he was going to die. Coming out alive was like getting a new life. "There will never be a more powerful experience," he said.

To get back to his car, Ralston had to rappel down a 60-foot (18-m) cliff face. After hiking a while, he ran into a family of three. They gave him water and helped him keep going toward the trailhead where they could get help. But Ralston's parents had reported him missing, so authorities were already looking for him. When his rescuers called for help on their cell phone, a search-and-rescue helicopter was already in the area. It arrived quickly to take Ralston to a nearby hospital.

At first Ralston was determined not to let the horrific experience change who he was. After he recovered and got a

DID YOU KNOW?

Ralston surprised the EMTs and hospital staff when he walked from the helicopter into the hospital. They assumed he would not have the strength after what he had been through. They were expecting to take him in a wheelchair

Ralston later became a motivational speaker. He continues to pursue wilderness adventures.

prosthetic arm, he got right back to taking dangerous hikes. He also took up the extreme sport of ultrarunning—running very long distances, often more than 100 miles (160 km) at a time.

Ralston finished his goal of hiking all the fourteeners alone in winter. He said he felt invincible. Since he had survived the ordeal in Utah, he believed, nothing could hurt him.

It wasn't until a woman he loved broke up with him that he came crashing down to earth. That same year, he lost three friends to suicide. Ralston was crushed, depressed, and suicidal. In the depths of this low period, he reevaluated his priorities and realized that human relationships are where life's meaning comes from.

He got help for his depression, and the next year he met another woman. Her name was Jessica. The two were married in 2009, and soon they had a son, Leo.

Aron Ralston still likes being alone in the wilderness. But he likes playing with his son even more.

IN THE MOUNTAIN OF THE SLEEPING LADY
THE WILD BOARS SOCCER TEAM

Those who live in northern Thailand share a legend about Doi Nang Non, or "The Mountain of the Sleeping Lady." They say that there was a beautiful princess who fell in love with a stable boy. Because their love was forbidden, they ran away together and hid in a cave. Eventually the princess became pregnant. Later, when the boy snuck out of the cave to find food, the king's soldiers captured and killed him. When the princess found out, she was so devastated that she took a long hairpin from her hair and stabbed herself to death. According to the legend, her body became the mountain. If you look at the mountain range from a distance, you can see the shape of a pregnant woman.

The mountain contains a system of caves that fill with water during the wet season. The legend says that these waters are the princess's blood.

That was the mountain—and those were the caves—that the Wild Boars soccer team decided to explore on Saturday, June 23, 2018. They didn't know that those legendary waters would change their lives forever.

A KIND OF FAMILY

The Wild Boars were a close-knit team of boys who practiced hard and spent much of their free time together. They liked to challenge themselves, and many times after practice their coach would take them on adventures involving swimming, bicycling, or exploring.

The coach who led them on this adventure was 25-year-old Ekkaphon Chanthawong. The kids called him Coach Ek. Ek's parents had died when he was 12, and he went to live in a monastery, where he trained to be a monk. He left the monastery when he was 22 to take care of his sick grandmother. Though he had given up life in the monkhood by the time he was hired to help coach the Wild Boars, he was still a devout Buddhist. He meditated regularly.

Ek coached the younger kids in the club, so he recruited some of the older kids to help out on the journey. After practice Ek and 12 boys gathered food and water for a long afternoon adventure.

The boys of the Wild Boars soccer team visited England for a training session.

Then they got on their bikes and tackled the Mountain of the Sleeping Lady. It was a hard, steep climb, but they had biked up harder mountains before. They loved the challenge.

When they reached the mouth of the cave, they saw a sign that warned them about rising water levels during the wet season. But the wet season didn't usually begin for another week or more, so they decided it was safe to go inside. The boys and their coach left their bikes along a railing outside the cave and went in. It was dark, and in many areas the boys had to crawl through tight passageways. The cave system was more than 6 miles (10 km) long.

Not long after they entered, a hard and sudden rainstorm erupted. The caves began to fill with water.

The entrance to the cave is in a forest in northern Thailand.

RISING WATERS—AND CONCERNS

That evening the team's head coach began to receive phone calls from parents wondering where their children were. They should have been home already. The head coach, Nopparat Khanthawong, tried calling Coach Ek but couldn't reach him. He tried several of the players who were with Coach Ek. But nobody was getting cell service in the caves. Finally, growing nervous, Khanthawong went up the mountain to the cave entrance. He saw the boys' bicycles. He also saw water spilling out of the cave. Khanthawong stood at the mouth of the cave and screamed, "Ek! Ek! Ek!" But there was no answer.

Khanthawong felt his body turn cold. This was not good. He called the authorities.

Inside the cave, floodwaters cut off the boys and their coach from returning the way they had come in. As the water rose, they were forced to go deeper into the maze of tunnels, searching for higher ground to avoid drowning.

Rain continued to fall into the next day, when police and park officials began searching the cave system. They found handprints and footprints that they believed belonged to the boys, but they couldn't search farther due to the flooding water. So they called in Royal Thai Navy SEAL divers. The divers plunged into the flooded cave carrying oxygen tanks and food for the boys. But the water was muddy, making it hard to see even with lights. One of the divers described it as swimming through cold coffee.

Outside the cave, families gathered and waited desperately for news. Some set up shrines and prayed.

The water in the cave wasn't only dirty and hard to see through. It was also rushing fast, making things even more difficult. And, although the Navy SEALs were world-class divers, they didn't have much experience diving in caves. The situation seemed impossible, but nobody was giving up. The next day more help arrived—three British diving experts and 30 American military personnel, including survival experts.

The British experts, among the best divers in the world, went into the cave. But with waters rushing violently and visibility at zero, they had to retreat.

TOO MUCH WATER

The next day, the fifth day the boys had been underground, the operation expanded further. Huge pumps were installed to start pumping water out of the caves. Experts built a large, improvised dam to divert water from the cave. Up the mountain, in the thick jungle above the caves, teams used drones, robots, and sniffer dogs to search for a "chimney"—an alternative shaft through which the team might be reached. They found two chimneys and drilled into one that led to a muddy chamber. But the lost soccer team was not there. In a nearby swimming pool, divers practiced evacuation drills to use for the players if they were found.

DID YOU KNOW?

At one point it was estimated that the pumps were removing about 420,000 gallons (1.6 million liters) per hour from the cave. All the water removed by the pumps and the dam flowed into nearby farm fields and destroyed crops.

Teams of helpers worked to remove water from the flooded cave.

Still more divers from around the world arrived to help out. But all the divers, with all their expertise, ran into the same problems: visibility and current. One after another they plunged into the cave, fighting the current and feeling their way along, and then returned, having explored around 330 feet (100 m). Some said they should give up the search. It was too dangerous, and they feared someone would be killed. Instead, they kept working. The divers went in and laid down guidelines that could be followed in the dark, getting farther with each attempt.

Finally, after the soccer team had been trapped for a full week, the rescuers caught a break. The rains stopped. For now, at least, less mud was being stirred up, so visibility was better. With the lines they had already laid, the divers were able to make quicker headway. They worked in shifts—one team would go down, searching and laying more line, while others slept.

The rain ending was a good sign, but it did not relieve all the pressure on the rescuers. The wet season was just around the corner, and heavy monsoons were predicted in a matter of days. So the rescue teams set up a base in a dry room inside the cave with fresh tanks and other supplies. That allowed them to stay underground longer. Each dive lasted six to eight hours. When the divers returned to the surface, they were exhausted.

INSIDE: A FOCUS ON CALM

The rescuers and the families of the boys had no idea what was happening with the team, or if they were still alive. But they were. Deep inside the cave, Coach Ek was doing everything he could to keep the boys safe. He and his players were sitting on a rocky ledge above a pool of water about 2.5 miles (4 km) from the cave entrance. Ek shared his own food among the kids to keep them healthy. He showed them how to drink water that dripped from the sides of the cave and not the water in the pool, which was much dirtier and could make them very sick.

Ek helped the players stay calm by teaching them to meditate. Being trapped in the dark, not knowing if anyone would find them, would be terrifying for anyone. But Ek knew that the ancient practice of Buddhist meditation was an effective tool for achieving peace of mind and freedom from suffering. By teaching his players to meditate, Ek was able to keep them from panicking.

Meanwhile, the divers were making progress, but they had run into a new problem. Specifically, they had run into a sharp turn that led into a very narrow passageway. Diver Ben Reymenants and his team finally got through and laid 1,300 more feet (396 m) of guidelines.

The rescue effort, lead by the Navy SEALs of Thailand, involved a dangerous dive and a 2-mile (3.7-km) swim through murky water.

After getting through the tight junction, Reymenants had a good idea what room the lost players might be in. But he ran out of line and had to turn around. When he got back to the base, a team of British divers was getting ready to go in. Reymenants told the Brits that they were very close. "You probably can find them," he said. The Brits—Richard Stanton and John Volanthen—followed the lines to the end and kept going, laying more line as they went.

THRILLING DISCOVERY

Within three hours, Volanthen surfaced in a dark room deep inside the cave. He cast a flashlight around the room, and he was thrilled with what he saw: the boys and their coach, many of them smiling and chattering. The team had been found!

"Hey you, thank you, thank you," the boys called out.

The first thing Volanthen did was ask how many were with them. They confirmed that all 13 were there. "Thirteen. Brilliant," Volanthen replied. The players asked if they were going to be rescued now, but Volanthen had to tell them that it would take time. "Not today," he said. But he assured them the rescue would be starting.

He video-recorded the boys to show everyone when he returned from the cave. On the video, the boys appear healthy and in good spirits. They asked what day it was, and Volanthen told them it was Monday. "You have been here 10 days," he said. "You are very strong, very strong."

Outside the cave, families and rescuers reacted with joy that the boys had been found. They cheered and thrust their fists into the air.

Of course, the rescuers still had to figure out how to get the boys out. Many plans were discussed. One was to bring in enough food for four months—the amount of time they thought it would take to teach the boys how to scuba dive out of the cave. But the route was perilous even for the experts. It was unlikely the boys could learn enough to navigate the dangerous passageway, even with training. Most of them couldn't even swim. And, as one of the rescue consultants said, it would be "a truly terrifying experience" for the boys. They were weak and exhausted from being trapped for so long, which would make the job even harder.

Additionally, there was more rain in the forecast, and oxygen levels in the cave were dropping. Rescuers had to get them out fast. They decided they had no choice but for the divers to take out each member of the team one by one.

Saman Kunan

Four Thai Navy SEAL divers give thumbs up to indicate that all the boys were rescued.

The effort involved 90 expert divers—40 from Thailand and 50 others from around the world. Some were dispatched into the cave to prepare the boys on the Wild Boars team. They included four Thai divers, an army doctor, and three Thai Navy SEALs.

DARING RESCUE

Finally, on July 8, after the Wild Boars had been trapped for more than two weeks, rescuers were ready to start taking them out. Four boys were fitted with wet suits and oxygen tanks, and full-face masks were sealed onto their faces with silicone to keep them secure. The doctor gave the boys a sedative to knock them out so they would not panic during the scary journey. Their hands were bound behind their backs and their feet bound together so that, if they did wake, they wouldn't tear off the masks in panic and drown.

Then each boy was strapped to a diver. A 14-year-old nicknamed Note was the first to go out. The team got him through the first underwater section to a beach inside the cave where they checked his health. Then they continued, carrying Note over dry parts and diving through underwater passages. The journey out took several hours.

All four boys made it out safely that first day. Four more were rescued the next day. On the third day, the final four players and Coach Ek were successfully rescued from the cave. All were taken directly to a hospital in the nearest city, Chiang Rai.

The boys didn't know it while they were trapped underground, but their ordeal had become an international story. People everywhere were riveted by the daring rescue mission, which even the expert divers had labeled as nearly impossible. Now the Mountain of the Sleeping Lady has a new legend—the rescue of the Wild Boars.

ALONE AGAINST THE ARCTIC
ADA BLACKJACK

Ada Blackjack had done it for her son—her only surviving child. Five-year-old Bennett had been ill with tuberculosis, but she couldn't afford basic needs, much less the doctors and medical attention he required. So she had put him into an orphanage. In order to earn the money she needed to take him home and care for him, she undertook a dangerous journey. Now she didn't know if she would ever see him again. She was stranded on a remote, frozen island in the Arctic Ocean. Supplies were low, and she was all alone.

Well, not quite alone. She had a cat. Fierce polar bears wandered the icy landscape. There was also the dead man in the shelter.

Born in a tiny village called Spruce Creek, Alaska, Ada was sent to live with Methodist missionaries in the mining town of Nome after her father died when she was eight. The missionaries taught her writing and math as well as skills such as cooking, cleaning, and sewing. It was this last skill that would land her on a ship bound for Wrangel Island years later.

Ada married Jack Blackjack, a musher and hunter, when she was 16. She had three children with him, but he treated her terribly. He beat her, starved her, and eventually left her on the Seward Peninsula, where they were living. Their first two children had died, and the third, Bennett, was sick. Abandoned and, as she later told a reporter, "bone poor," she had no choice but to return to Nome, which was 40 miles (64 km) away. She walked, carrying Bennett much of the way. Soon after, she placed him in the orphanage.

When Blackjack heard of the expedition to Wrangel Island, she decided to take the chance. It paid $50 a month, which was far more than she could earn in town. She would be gone for two years, but when she returned, she and Bennett would be reunited. He could have the medical attention he needed and the mother and the life that he deserved.

Ada Blackjack and her son, Bennett, 1923

A GRAND EXPEDITION

The trip was arranged by Canadian explorer Vilhjalmur Stefansson, who hoped to claim the island for Britain. Stefansson himself did not go on the trip. He assembled the supplies and the ship, the *Silver Wave*. He also hired a crew of four: Americans Frederick Maurer, E. Lorne Knight, and Milton Galle; and Canadian Allan Crawford. Also on the trip was a cat named Victoria. The crew decided to hire some local Inupiat people to help maintain camp and cook.

Blackjack was the only Inupiat who showed up. Being raised by the Christian missionaries meant that she hadn't learned traditional Inupiat skills such as hunting and wilderness survival. But she could cook, and—more importantly—she could sew. The men needed her to make and maintain their boots and other gear.

The *Silver Wave* left Nome on September 9, 1921, with six months of supplies for what they expected to be their two-year stay on Wrangel Island. That was the length of time required to stake claim to unoccupied land. The idea was that they would hunt for meat to add to their supplies until a ship came the following summer with more. They had a team of dogs and a sled that they would use to hunt.

A GLOOMY WELCOME

Wrangel Island was draped in fog when they landed on September 16 and unloaded their supplies. The ocean around it froze solid for most of the year, only opening up for a short time during the warmer months. It was a desolate, forbidding place. As the ship disappeared on the horizon on its way back to Alaska, Blackjack walked away down the beach. She didn't want the men to see her cry.

Anthropologist and explorer Vilhjalmur Stefansson published more than 20 books about his travels in the Arctic.

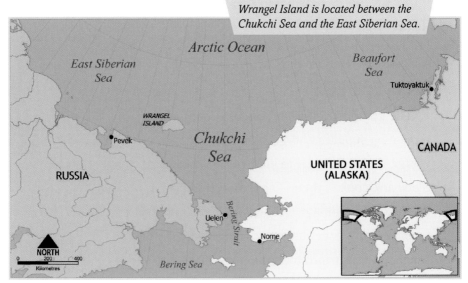

Wrangel Island is located between the Chukchi Sea and the East Siberian Sea.

"I thought at first that I would turn back," she later said. But she decided it wouldn't be fair to the men she was traveling with.

They got to work. At first they lived in tents, but eventually they constructed a snow house. Blackjack sewed hoods to the men's reindeer parkas. The men set up weather instruments and hunted geese and polar bears. In the evenings Blackjack sang hymns and Crawford told jokes. The hunting was plentiful, and for several months, things went well.

The following summer, Knight went off by himself to explore. He went swimming in the Skeleton River, and this may have affected his health. He was never well again after that swim.

Meanwhile, the crew began to worry about two things. One, the game seemed to disappear. Although the hunting had been good for many months, now they rarely saw animals to hunt. The second thing that worried them was that the resupply ship hadn't come when expected. As summer turned to fall, and ice re-formed in the bays, they realized the ship was not going to make it.

Stefansson had hired a ship, the *Teddy Bear*. But an ice storm had struck the island in June and frozen the ocean surrounding Wrangel. It was impossible for the *Teddy Bear* to get through.

GOING FOR HELP

The group on the island rationed out their remaining supplies and prepared for a long, hard winter. They managed to kill two walruses, and Blackjack cooked them. Otherwise, they had little success hunting. They celebrated Christmas together, but by the new year, things were desperate. Knight and Crawford took the dogs and left to see if they could get across the frozen Chukchi Sea to Siberia. There they could get help. But they returned in only a couple weeks because Knight felt fatigued and stiff.

Knight knew he was sick, and he turned angry and moody. He had scurvy, a disease that comes from not getting enough vitamin C. It can be deadly if it goes untreated long enough. Blackjack knew she would have to take care of him.

But first, in minus 56 degrees Fahrenheit (minus 49 degrees Celsius), she helped the other three men pack the sled so they could go for help. They took many of the team's precious remaining supplies, but they believed it was their best hope. The men said they would return with help, either by ship or with another team of dogs and more supplies.

The stranded explorers made camp in canvas tents on the tundra of Wrangel Island.

They left on January 29. Blackjack was alone with the dying Knight, and the next day an ominous and massive storm moved in. The three men were never seen again.

By February, Knight was unable to get out of bed. Blackjack kept a warm bag of sand by his feet and sewed pillows out of oatmeal sacks and cotton to comfort him. But he got worse. He felt helpless and angry. He took out his anger on Blackjack, criticizing her for not doing a better job of taking care of him. But Blackjack, who had never hunted or chopped wood before, had learned quickly how to do these things and tend to Knight's health.

When she was with him, Blackjack remained cheerful and positive. But she wrote in her diary, "He never . . . [thinks] how . . . hard [it is] for [a woman] to take four [men's] place, to . . . work and to [hunt] for something to eat for him . . ."

FIGHTING FOR LIFE

She was determined to keep him alive, hunting every day. Her aim with the gun was still not good, and most days she couldn't shoot anything. Sometimes she brought home a goose or seagull. Other times she gathered roots to make a stew. But Knight's health continued to decline.

Late in the spring, it was clear that Knight was going to die. Blackjack was afraid that she would be left alone. Looking down at him, she began to cry, but Knight assured her that she had done her best to save him. He thanked her for all she had done.

He died on June 23. Blackjack didn't have the strength to bury Knight, so she left him in his bed and built a barricade of storage boxes around him to keep wild animals away. To get away from the smell of decay, she moved out of the snow house and into the storage tent. She insulated it with driftwood and kept a gun by the door in case polar bears attacked.

Wrangel Island is a common breeding ground for polar bears in the Arctic.

Blackjack had grown up hearing Inupiat myths about polar bears. The legends called the polar bear "the great lonely roamer." It was wise, powerful, and, according to some legends, it was a half-human creature that could shed its bear skin when alone. It could talk, and it could capture the souls of those who hunted it. With these stories haunting her, she was terrified of polar bears.

But she was determined to survive so she could see her son again. *I must stay alive*, she thought. *I will live.*

LEARNING, WORKING, AND HOPING

Blackjack learned how to set traps to catch game such as white foxes. She built a small boat from driftwood and canvas. The men had left behind their photography equipment, and she figured out how to use it. She took pictures of herself standing outside of camp. At night she dreamed she was surrounded by people.

Blackjack became more skilled with the gun, and she managed to shoot a few seals. Fearing polar bears, she built a platform above her shelter so that she could spot them from far away. One day she had a very close call. She had shot a seal and was preparing to take it back to the tent when she saw a mother polar bear and her cub. She was 400 yards (365 m) from her tent, and she ran as hard as she could to get there, leaving the seal behind. She climbed to her platform and, using binoculars, looked out toward her seal. The mother

Expedition member Lorne Knight searched the horizon for a rescue ship.

and her cub were devouring it. She fired her gun in anger, but she was glad it was not her that the bears were eating.

DID YOU KNOW?

Wrangel Island is now part of Russia. It is designated

Blackjack chewed sealskins to soften them so she could mold them into new soles for her boots. She knitted new fingers for her gloves, and she made a reindeer parka. And she practiced shooting. Since she didn't know whether she would be rescued before winter, it was important to be ready.

At night she heard the sound of the ice pack around the island crashing and shifting. More than once, she woke up to find that a polar bear had been in her camp. But Blackjack kept her wits. She wrote in her diary that it was the cat, Victoria, that helped her the most. She talked to Victoria all the time, and she said she thought she'd have gone insane without her.

In August the ice pack cleared, and Blackjack watched for a rescue ship. She used her new boat to go duck hunting on the open water. On the night of August 19, she dreamed about a ship. When she woke up, she saw that the fire had gone out. While she built it back up, she heard a rumbling sound outside—probably the walrus that often bobbed up in the bay there. She ate a breakfast of dried duck and seal oil. But the noise outside grew louder.

Finally Blackjack went up to her platform and scanned the bay with her binoculars. Everything was shrouded in fog, and she couldn't see anything. Then the fog shifted. She saw something moving.

It was the mast of a ship.

Blackjack was saved. She returned home on the ship and was paid, though she was given less than she'd been promised. But she had enough to take her son to Seattle to have his tuberculosis treated. Her story became international news, and Stefansson, the man who had set up the deadly trip, made money from the venture.

But Blackjack didn't want any attention. She said she was not special—she was just a mother who wanted to get home to her son.

A NIGHT IN THE
DEATH ZONE
BECK WEATHERS

Most people would consider Beck Weathers a very lucky
guy—even *before* he survived a harrowing near-death experience
on the highest mountain in the world. He had a successful career
as a pathologist—a doctor who studies how diseases affect our
bodies. He had money. He lived in a comfortable suburb of Dallas,
Texas. He was married with two kids, and he loved his family.

But Weathers didn't feel lucky. He felt empty. He felt like
something was missing. Weathers had
depression—he called it "the black dog."
At times he thought of suicide.

Instead, he threw himself into activities
to try to fill the empty space inside him. He
became interested in CB radios, motorcycling,
and sailing. And then, when he was 40, he took
a climbing trip in Rocky Mountain National
Park. From then on, he was hooked on
mountain climbing. Climbing was the one thing
that gave him true peace and happiness. When
you're climbing, he said, "Everything else in
your entire life disappears, and it's just one step
after the other."

*To climb to the top of Mount
Everest, the world's highest
mountain, is a goal for many
of the world's best climbers.*

CLIMBING AWAY FROM THE BLACK DOG

Weathers tried to beat his depression symptoms by replacing them with something else: an obsession with climbing. He became consumed with reaching higher and higher goals—literally. He vowed to climb the Seven Summits, the highest peak on each of the seven continents, and he trained intensely. Every day, he woke up at 4 a.m. to exercise, in his words, "like an animal," and then he went to work at the hospital. When he came home at night, he barely talked to his family. He collapsed into bed, exhausted, by 8 p.m. He took long trips without his family to exotic locations, checking those mountain peaks off his list.

By the spring of 1996, Weathers had climbed five of the Seven Summits. Mount Everest was to be the second-to-last one. At 29,029 feet (8,848 m) above sea level, it is the highest mountain peak in the world. Airplanes typically cruise at about 30,000 feet (9,000 m), just a thousand feet higher. About 150 climbers had died on the mountain, which is nestled in the Himalayas along the border between China and Nepal.

Weathers's mental health may have improved, but his marriage was suffering. His wife, Peach, said climbing was ruining their relationship. Before Weathers left for Everest that March, she told him that she would divorce him after he returned. And so, as Weathers arrived in Nepal, his marriage in ruins, he was prepared to push himself to the absolute limit. He felt he had nothing left to lose.

Three teams would be climbing together. Weathers's team, Adventure Consultants, was led by Rob Hall and included two other guides, Mike Groom and Andy Harris. There were eight clients, including Weathers and the author Jon Krakauer, who was researching an article for *Outdoor* magazine. Eight Nepalese Sherpas were also part of the expedition.

DID YOU KNOW?

After Krakauer's article appeared in *Outdoor* magazine, he expanded it into a book, *Into Thin Air*, which became a best seller. It was made into a TV movie one year later. In 1998 a documentary film called *Everest* was produced, which

The climb was broken down into camps, each higher than the previous. Base Camp was lowest, then Camp One, Camp Two, Camp Three, and Camp Four. The summit was about 3,000 feet (900 m) above Camp Four.

POOR SIGHT FOR SORE EYES

The teams began climbing on March 31, 1996, passing through villages on their way to Base Camp. They took it slowly, allowing everyone to adjust to the altitude. Since they had all come from sea level, the thin, oxygen-poor air made strenuous activity like climbing difficult. Many felt sick until they acclimated. Weathers noticed that he was having problems with his vision. He had recently undergone surgery to correct his nearsightedness. The altitude was causing his corneas to change shape, making it a struggle for him to see.

On April 10 the group arrived at Base Camp, about 17,600 feet (5,360 m) above sea level. It was about −10°F (−23°C), fairly warm for that altitude. They spent a couple of weeks there acclimating and preparing to climb higher.

In mid-April they began to climb again. The plan was to climb about 2,000 feet (610 m) up and establish Camp One. Then another 2,000 feet to Camp Two, another 2,000 feet to Camp Three, and finally 2,000 more feet to Camp Four. Each time they carried camping and climbing gear, tanks of oxygen, and food and water up to a higher camp, they returned to lower elevations to rest and regain their strength. Spending short periods of time at the higher altitudes helped them gradually adjust to them.

Along the way, they had to climb a part of the mountain called the Icefall. It was a glacier resting over a drop-off. Because the glacier moves a few feet every day, huge nails of ice form along it, making it an especially treacherous climb. Hikers use ladders and ropes, which

With permits, guides, and other expenses, the cost of attempting to climb Mount Everest can be more than $45,000 per person.

have been attached to the ice by Sherpas, to climb the beautiful but deadly structure. Over the years before Weathers and his team got there, 18 climbers had died on the Icefall.

DEATH NEAR THE SUMMIT

By May 6 the teams were ready to attempt the summit. They left Camp Three on May 9 and, wearing down suits and sucking on oxygen tanks, trudged toward Camp Four. The wind began to pick up, making conditions even colder and harsher. That afternoon, a climber from another expedition, Chen Yu-Nan, slipped and fell into a crevasse. At first he called out that he was okay. But within hours, he was dead.

The Sherpas took this as a bad sign and did not want to continue. But that night, the wind eased up and the sky was beautiful and clear. Weathers and the others looked up at the stars in the wide sky. They made the decision to press onward to the summit.

The area above Camp Four is known as the Death Zone. The oxygen level there is one-third the oxygen level at sea level, causing the human brain not to work as well as it usually does. With headlamps lighting up cones of the icy landscape in front of them, the climbers continued on. They used their ice axes to help get leverage for every step, breathing from their oxygen canisters as they went.

Team leader Rob Hall had everyone meet in a spot known as the Balcony. They started early so they would have plenty of time to reach the summit and return to camp before dark. As they waited for everyone to arrive, the sun rose, lighting up the valley. The sun, with its warmth and light, was a welcome sight to Weathers. But that high up, with the climbers working so hard, the heat and light of the blazing sun drained energy. Weathers knew that they had to reach the summit and get back down soon.

However, the rising sun also revealed that the altitude had worsened Weathers's vision troubles. Hall told him that he could not continue, and Weathers agreed with the decision. He was content to have gotten as far as he had. So he reclined in the snow, relaxing in the sun. Now he only had to wait for the others to return on their way down and get back to camp.

"Sitting there was almost like a day at the beach," he said later. "If I'd had a lounge chair, then it would have been perfect, because you're very warm, it's pleasant, there's no wind, you've got this incredible view."

A LONG WAIT

Many of the climbers continued toward the summit, while others turned back. Oxygen tanks were running low, and fatigue was setting in. The sun was like a clock ticking down—nobody wanted to be up near the summit when it got dark again. Navigating down the mountain in the dark with little or no oxygen and feeling more tired than they did going up could be a deadly combination. Weathers continued to wait for his guide and the others to return.

By about 3 p.m. climbers were still going up and down the narrow pathway to the summit, creating a bottleneck. The sun

Everest Base Camp

would be setting soon, and Hall still had not returned for Weathers. Weathers's vision was worsening, and he was starting to worry. As the sun set, temperatures dropped fast. Weathers began to shiver and hallucinate. He was developing hypothermia.

Jon Krakauer, on his way down from the summit, stopped and told Weathers that Hall was stuck on the summit ridge. Krakauer offered to help Weathers get down, but Weathers decided to wait for Mike Groom, another guide from his team. Groom arrived soon after and helped Weathers and several others make their way down to a pass known as the South Col. They were near Camp Four, but a harsh wind was picking up. The sky, which had been clear all day, was now crowded with heavy clouds that were starting to dump snow on the group.

The swirling conditions were disorienting. One hiker compared it to "being lost in a bottle of milk." They had a close call when they nearly walked off a ledge. In the confusion, Weathers lost a glove. He had taken it off to warm his hand under his jacket, but the wind ripped it from his hand, and it vanished. Weathers's hand froze the minute it was exposed to the frigid air.

Without any way to see, and knowing they could plummet off the side of the mountain at any moment, the group decided to huddle and wait. They stayed as close to one another as they could to share warmth. Maybe the storm would die down and they could find the tents. Or maybe someone would find them. Meanwhile, they were trapped in the Death Zone.

The wind blasted them with ice. They yelled at one another and pounded on one another's backs to stay awake, knowing that even a minute of sleep could lead to a deadly hypothermic coma. They flapped their arms and legs to stay warm, and they tried to keep their thoughts positive in spite of the brutal pain.

LEFT FOR DEAD

Weathers's condition was getting worse. At some point during the height of the storm, crazed not only from hypothermia but also oxygen deficiency, he stood up and yelled, "I've got this all figured out!" The wind battered him as he raised his exposed, frozen hand in the air, and he fell into the whiteout. The group knew they could never find him in these conditions. They assumed he would die quickly.

During a brief break in the storm, those in the huddle who had strength got up and somehow found their way to Camp Four. They sent hikers from the camp back to find Weathers and the others who were left behind. One of the guides from another team, Anatoli Boukreev, eventually found them. But Boukreev took one look at Weathers and realized he was virtually dead. There was no point wasting precious energy carrying him back to the camp.

The next morning others were sent to find missing climbers. This group located Weathers, half-buried in the snow, his frozen arm protruding into the air. One of the searchers was a doctor who determined that Weathers was alive but wouldn't live much longer. Nobody had ever recovered from a hypothermic coma before. As Boukreev had done, they left him. When they got back to camp, they radioed to Base Camp that Weathers was dead. His wife was called.

But after the doctor left, something incredible happened. Weathers woke up. He looked at his frozen arm and realized he was on the mountain, and he was close to death. *If I don't get up,* he thought, *if I don't stand, if I don't start thinking about where I am and how to get out of there, then this is going to be over very quickly.*

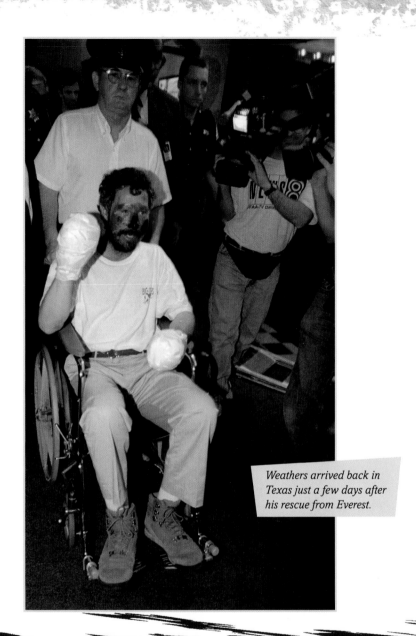

Weathers arrived back in Texas just a few days after his rescue from Everest.

DID YOU KNOW?

Eight people died during that storm near the summit of Mount Everest, including three guides. One was the Adventure Consultants expedition leader, Rob Hall.

LEFT FOR DEAD—AGAIN

Somehow, he stumbled along the South Col and into Camp Four. To the other hikers there, who had assumed he was dead, he looked like a ghost. His face was black with frostbite. They helped him into a tent and made him as comfortable as they could. But they expected that he would be dead by morning.

In the morning, though, Weathers was still very much alive. By that time, rescuers had arrived to help him and the others down to Base Camp. Weathers was airlifted to a hospital. He had surgery to remove parts of both his arms, one foot, and much of his face. The frostbite had penetrated the cartilage of his nose and gone into his skull. Before the surgeon removed his dead nose, he took an impression of it. Then doctors made a new one in the same shape on his forehead, and when it was complete, they put it in place of the old one.

Weathers returned to his wife, Peach, who decided to stay with him for a year while he recovered from his injuries. During that time the two grew close again, thanks to Weathers's newfound appreciation for life—and for his own self-worth. "For the first time in my life, I have peace," he said. "I no longer seek to define myself externally, through goals and achievements and material possessions. For the first time, I'm comfortable in my own skin."

In 2015 Weathers attended the premiere of the movie Everest, *which was based on his expedition.*

DROPPED INTO THE AMAZON
JULIANE KOEPCKE

The last thing Juliane Koepcke remembered was seeing the treetops of the Peruvian rain forest spinning toward her. From where she was, high in the air, she thought they looked like broccoli.

"I was in a free fall, strapped to my [airplane] seat bench and hanging head over heels," she said. "The whispering of the wind was the only noise I could hear."

A bolt of lightning had struck the small turboprop airplane Juliane had been flying in, blowing up an engine and tearing off the wing. The plane and its 91 passengers went into a nosedive, and the air filled with screams. The air also filled with a flurry of flying Christmas presents. It was Christmas Eve, 1971. Juliane was 17 years old.

HOLIDAY GONE WRONG

Juliane and her mother were flying to the town of Pucallpa, Peru, in the Amazonian rain forest. Her father was there, and they were eager to spend Christmas with him. Both her parents were famous zoologists. They ran a research station in the jungle and studied wildlife.

Juliane plummeted 2 miles (3.2 km) to earth, crashing into those trees in the jungle. When she woke the next morning, she was alone—deep in the rain forest of Peru. One of her eyes was swollen shut. She had a concussion and couldn't sit up. She drifted in and out of consciousness. She later said it felt like "being wrapped in cotton balls." Miraculously, her only injuries other than the concussion were a broken collarbone, a torn knee ligament, and cuts and bruises.

When Juliane finally felt strong enough to get up, she realized that she was underneath her airplane seat. Somehow she had come unbuckled. At some point after the crash, she had crawled under the seat to avoid rain. Now she crawled out and called to her mother, who had been sitting next to her on the plane. She got no response.

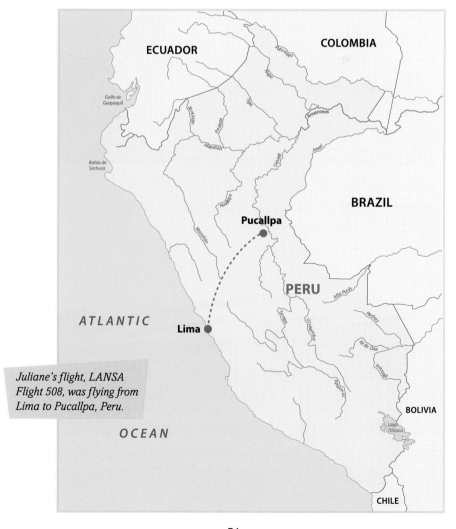

Juliane's flight, LANSA Flight 508, was flying from Lima to Pucallpa, Peru.

Struggling to stay conscious, Juliane searched for her mother and other survivors. But there was no one. No voices answered her calls. She saw no bodies. Overhead, she heard the buzzing sound of rescue planes looking for the crash, but she couldn't see them. The planes couldn't see her either through the dense rain forest canopy. Her heart sank. If they could not see the crash site, they would not keep looking for her.

She was wearing only a short, sleeveless dress and one sandal. She had also lost her eyeglasses, making it hard for her to see much in front of her. She did find a small bag of candy. It was her only source of food, but she was determined to find her way out of the jungle alive.

DID YOU KNOW?

The climate in this part of Peru is very warm and stays mostly the same year-round. In December the average high temperature is about 89°F (32°C). The average low is just over 72°F (22°C).

A Lockheed aircraft similar to the one that crashed in the Amazon

AMAZON EXPERT

In a way, Juliane had been in training for being alone in the jungle for much of her life. Her parents had moved to Peru to study tropical wildlife, and she was born there in 1954. She grew up learning about the wonders and mysteries of the rain forest from her parents. Before the crash, she had spent a year and a half living at her parents' research station, just 30 miles (48 km) away.

From her parents, Juliane had learned of the jungle's worst dangers. She knew that spiders, mosquitoes, and snakes were her biggest threats. Since she was having trouble seeing without her glasses, she used her one remaining sandal to test the path in front of her for snakes and other creeping hazards before taking each step.

She also remembered many survival strategies her father had taught her. She remembered that walking in water can be safer than walking on the jungle floor, which was crawling with poison plants. He also taught her that if you are lost in the jungle, heading downhill will likely lead to a stream or river. And a stream or river will likely lead to civilization.

When Juliane found a small creek, she began to follow it. It led to a larger stream. She waded in and walked as close to the

Dense vegetation in the Peruvian rain forest made hiking difficult.

middle as she could. One thing she worried about was piranhas—carnivorous fish that lurked in the waterways of the Amazon. But she knew that piranhas were less likely to school in the middle of the stream. Sometimes she saw crocodiles on the banks, but she was less afraid of them. Her father had taught her that they rarely attacked humans.

One thing she couldn't protect herself from was the infection growing in her wounds. At night the pain of infected insect bites left her unable to sleep. And on her upper right arm, she had a small wound that flies had laid eggs in. The maggots had hatched and were eating into her arm. She knew she had to get them out or her arm might need to be amputated—if she ever got out of the jungle. She tried scraping them out with a stick, but it didn't work.

A TERRIBLE DISCOVERY

She floated downstream on the river as much as she could and walked when she couldn't. On the fourth day, she heard a familiar sound. It was the powerful wing beats of a king vulture landing. The sound terrified her because she knew that those scavenger birds only landed on the ground for one reason—if there was a large dead body to eat. She assumed the birds had smelled the bodies of some of the other passengers from her flight.

When she came around a bend in the stream and saw a row of three attached airplane seats driven deep into the ground, she knew she had been right. She got closer and saw that the seats all had people in them, rammed down headfirst. Juliane paused there by the half-buried passengers from her flight.

She was especially terrified that one of the passengers might be her mother. But when she prodded the corpse with a stick, she saw that the woman had painted toenails. Her mother, she knew, never painted her toenails. She was relieved at first but then felt ashamed for feeling relief. The woman was, after all, somebody's loved one.

"I moved on after a while," she said, "but in the first moment after finding them, it was like I was paralyzed."

Juliane kept going, but with her injuries—and without water or food—she was becoming more and more delusional. She was in shock. It was hard to stand, but she forced herself to go on. She knew that nobody was going to save her. She had to save herself.

A HOPEFUL DISCOVERY

On the 10th day, she sank down along the riverbank. The afternoon was growing late, and she was thinking about finding a place to sleep for the night. She always tried to sleep on sloped ground or against a large tree so nothing could sneak up behind her. She was drifting in and out of sleep when suddenly, in a waking moment, she saw a boat.

It was right in front of her, moored on the river she was following. At first she thought she was hallucinating, but she went to it and reached out to touch it. She realized it was real, and a burst of adrenaline coursed through her. If there was a boat, there might be people nearby!

Juliane looked around and saw a small path near the boat. She followed the path up the hill, but it was hard work. She was so weak that she had to crawl. At the top of the path was a little hut with a roof and floor made of palm, but no walls. Under a tarp she found the motor to the boat and a barrel of diesel fuel.

When Juliane was younger, she'd had a dog that had gotten a cut. And, just like Juliane's, the cut had gotten infected with maggots. To get the maggots out, her dad had poured fuel into the cut. It was obviously extremely painful for the dog, but it worked. That was how they saved the dog's limb. And that was how Juliane knew she could save her own.

She found a tube and stuck it into the barrel. Then she sucked on it until the fuel started coming out, and she directed the stream onto her cut. The pain was intense, but she was able to pull out 30 maggots. She felt proud of herself for treating her wound, and as the sun went down, she turned her attention to finding food. There were frogs croaking all around her, and she tried to catch some to eat. Luckily, she wasn't quick enough—the frogs in that area were toxic and would have killed her. Starving and exhausted, she lay down to sleep under the tarp.

Juliane's knowledge of the plants and animals of the rain forest helped her survive.

Four months after the crash, Juliane moved to Germany to attend college.

FINDING HER RESCUERS

The next day Juliane heard voices approaching. She later said it was like hearing the voices of angels. It was three men.

"When they saw me, they were alarmed and stopped talking," she said. "They thought I was a kind of water goddess—a figure from local legend who is a hybrid of a water dolphin and a blonde, white-skinned woman."

Juliane introduced herself in Spanish to the shocked hunters. She explained that she had been in a plane crash. They had heard of the crash and began to help her. They treated her wounds and gave her some food. The next day they took her in their boat to a hospital downstream. In the town she met a local pilot who flew her to Pucallpa, the town where her father worked and where she and her mother had been flying. It was only a 15-minute flight, but Juliane was understandably nervous about getting into an airplane again. But her father was waiting for her, so she went.

"He could barely talk," she said of her dad when they reunited. "In the first moment, we just held each other."

With Juliane's directions, authorities were able to locate the crash site. They began to find bodies as well. No one else was found alive. When they found her mother, it hit home that Juliane had really lost her. Later, Juliane learned that her mother had also survived the fall. She had likely lived for several days, but she had been too injured to move. "I dread to think what her last days were like," Juliane said.

Juliane was suddenly famous. Everyone wanted to ask her about her ordeal. She was interviewed by magazines, and she received mail from around the world. The attention kept her busy—and distracted—for some time. She studied biology and, like her parents, grew up to be a scientist. But the question of how and why she was the only survivor of that terrible crash continues to haunt her.

GLOSSARY

acclimate—to get used to

amputate—to remove a part from the body

artery—a blood vessel that carries blood from the heart to the parts of the body

chimney—a narrow passage through rock

concussion—a brain injury that results from a hard blow to the head

decomposition—when tissue breaks down or decays

fourteener—a mountain with a peak higher than 14,000 feet (4,267 meters)

free-climbing—climbing something without using aids or supports such as ropes

hallucinate—to perceive objects (or people) that are not really there

hypothermia—a life-threatening condition that occurs when a person's body temperature becomes dangerously low

maggot—the larva of a fly

meditation—a mental exercise to relax the body and mind usually done by concentrating on one's breathing or repeating a mantra

missionary—a person who is sent by a religious group to teach that group's faith and do good works, especially in a foreign country

monastery—a group of buildings where monks live and work

monk—a man who lives in a religious community and has promised to devote his life to his religion

musher—a person who travels over snow with a sled drawn by dogs

rappel—to lower oneself down with a rope

scurvy—a disease caused by lack of vitamin C that causes great weakness and bleeding, especially of the gums

Sherpa—a person native to the Himalaya Mountains who guides people through the mountains

READ MORE

Aronson, Marc. *Rising Water: The Story of the Thai Cave Rescue.* New York: Atheneum Books for Young Readers, 2019.

Gifford, Clive. *The Ultimate Guide to Surviving in the Wild.* Minneapolis: Quarto Publishing, 2018.

Isaacs, Sally. *Helen Thayer's Arctic Adventure: A Woman and a Dog Walk to the North Pole.* North Mankato, MN: Capstone Young Readers, 2016.

INTERNET SITES

Backpacker: Survival Stories
https://www.backpacker.com/survival/survival-stories

GlacierWorks
http://glacierworks.org/

PBS Frontline: Storm over Everest
https://www.pbs.org/wgbh/pages/frontline/everest/etc/synopsis.html

SOURCE NOTES

p. 8, "I was accustomed…" Alex Hannaford, "127 Hours: Aron Ralston's Story of Survival," *The Telegraph*, January 6, 2011, https://www.telegraph.co.uk/culture/film/8223925/127-Hours-Aron-Ralstons-story-of-survival.html Accessed on April 18, 2019.

p. 8, "slow motion" Patrick Barkham, "The Extraordinary Story behind Danny Boyle's *127 Hours*," *The Guardian*, December 15, 2010, https://www.theguardian.com/film/2010/dec/15/story-danny-boyles-127-hours Accessed on April 18, 2019.

p. 10, "There's this surreal conversation…" Ibid.

p. 12, "I felt my bone bend…" Hannaford, "127 Hours: Aron Ralston's Story of Survival."

p. 12, "I had this huge grin…" Ibid.

p. 14, "There will never be…" "Aron Ralston Explains How He Cut off His Arm," NBC segment of Ted Koppel interview on YouTube, uploaded January 22, 2012, https://www.youtube.com/watch?v=3ud5i1_-nf0 Accessed on April 18, 2019.

p. 23, "You probably can find them" Radhika Viswanathan, "'This Is Madness': A Rescue Diver on What It Was Like to Save the Thai Boys in the Cave," *Vox*, July 12, 2018, https://www.vox.com/2018/7/12/17564360/thai-cave-rescue-boys-mission-diver-ben-reymenants Accessed on April 18, 2019.

p. 24, "Hey you…" Kocha Olarn and Lauren Said-Moorhouse, "Thai Cave Rescue: Soccer Team Found Alive One Kilometer Underground," CNN, July 3, 2018, https://edition.cnn.com/2018/07/02/asia/thai-cave-rescue-intl/index.html Accessed on April 18, 2019.

p. 24, "truly terrifying experience" Kocha Olarn and Lauren Said-Moorhouse, "Thai cave rescue…"

p. 28, "bone poor" "Death Vigil in Arctic Snows," *Los Angeles Times*, February 28, 1924, ProQuest Historical Newspapers, p. A1.

p. 32, "I thought at first…" Stephanie Buck, "Stranded for Two Years on an Arctic Island, This Woman Miraculously Survived by Shooting Seals," *Timeline*, August 29, 2017, https://timeline.com/ada-blackjack-stranded-island-4e6f0d2e198e Accessed on April 18, 2019.

p. 34, "He never…" Tessa Hulls, "Ada Blackjack, the Forgotten Sole Survivor of an Odd Arctic Expedition," *Atlas Obscura*, December 6, 2017, https://www.atlasobscura.com/articles/ada-blackjack-arctic-survivor Accessed on April 18, 2019.

p. 35, "the great lonely roamer" Jennifer Niven. *Ada Blackjack: A True Story of Survival in the Arctic*. New York: Hyperion, 2003.

p. 38, "the black dog" Eric Benson, "After Everest: The Complete Story of Beck Weathers," *Men's Journal*, n.d., https://www.mensjournal.com/adventure/after-everest-the-complete-story-of-beck-weathers-20150909 Accessed on April 18, 2019.

p. 38, "Everything else in…" Ibid.

p. 39, "like an animal" Beck Weathers. *Left for Dead: My Journey Home from Everest*. New York: Bantam, 2015, p. 4.

p. 43, "Sitting there…" "Stories—The Hour-by-Hour Unfolding Disaster | Storm over Everest," *PBS: Frontline*, https://www.pbs.org/wgbh/pages/frontline/everest/stories/unfolding.html Accessed on April 18, 2019.

p. 45, "being lost in a bottle of milk" Ed Douglas, "My life after death," *The Guardian*, October 21, 2000, https://www.theguardian.com/theobserver/2000/oct/22/focus.news Accessed on April 18, 2019.

p. 46, "I've got this all figured out!" Ibid.

p. 48, "For the first time…" Ibid.

p. 50, "I was in a free fall…" Juliane Koepcke, "How I Survived a Plane Crash," BBC News, March 24, 2012, https://www.bbc.com/news/magazine-17476615 Accessed on April 18, 2019.

p. 50, "being wrapped in cotton balls" Tim Littlewood, "The Woman Who Fell to Earth," *Vice*, September 2, 2010, https://www.vice.com/en_us/article/8gmgmz/the-woman-who-fell-to-earth-508-v17n9 Accessed on April 18, 2019.

p. 56, "I moved on after a while…" Ibid.

p. 58, "When they saw me…" Koepcke, "How I Survived a Plane Crash."

p. 59, "He could barely talk…" Ibid.

p. 59, "I dread to think…" Ibid.

SELECT BIBLIOGRAPHY

Books

Niven, Jennifer. *Ada Blackjack: A True Story of Survival in the Arctic*. New York: Hyperion, 2003.

Weathers, Beck. *Left for Dead: My Journey Home from Everest*. New York: Bantam, 2015.

Websites and Articles

"8 Saved, 5 to Go in Thai Cave Rescue," *New York Times*, July 9, 2018, https://www.nytimes.com/2018/07/09/world/asia/thailand-cave-rescue-live-updates.html Accessed on April 16, 2019.

Barkham, Patrick, "The Extraordinary Story behind Danny Boyle's *127 Hours*," *The Guardian*, December 15, 2010, https://www.theguardian.com/film/2010/dec/15/story-danny-boyles-127-hours Accessed on April 16, 2019.

Benson, Eric, "After Everest: The Complete Story of Beck Weathers," *Men's Journal*, n.d., https://www.mensjournal.com/adventure/after-everest-the-complete-story-of-beck-weathers-20150909 Accessed on April 16, 2019.

Berkeman, Oliver, "How I Snapped Bone and Cut off my Arm, by US Climber," *The Guardian*, May 9, 2003, https://www.theguardian.com/world/2003/may/09/usa.oliverburkeman Accessed on April 16, 2019.

Fedschun, Travis, "Thai Cave Boys Were Actually Handcuffed, Heavily Sedated During Dramatic Rescue, New Book Claims," *Fox News*, January 15, 2018, https://www.foxnews.com/world/thai-cave-boys-were-actually-handcuffed-heavily-sedated-during-dramatic-rescue-new-book-suggests Accessed on April 16, 2019.

Hulls, Tessa, "Ada Blackjack, the Forgotten Sole Survivor of an Odd Arctic Expedition," *Atlas Obscura*, December 6, 2017, https://www.atlasobscura.com/articles/ada-blackjack-arctic-survivor Accessed on April 16, 2019.

Koepcke, Juliane, "How I Survived a Plane Crash," *BBC News*, March 24, 2012, https://www.bbc.com/news/magazine-17476615 Accessed on April 16, 2019.

Littlewood, Tim, "The Woman Who Fell to Earth," *Vice*, September 2, 2010, https://www.vice.com/en_us/article/8gmgmz/the-woman-who-fell-to-earth-508-v17n9 Accessed on April 16, 2019.

Paddock, Richard C., "How Rescuers in a Thai Cave Pulled Off the Impossible," *New York Times*, July 10, 2018, https://www.nytimes.com/2018/07/10/world/asia/thailand-cave-rescue-how.html Accessed on April 16, 2019.

Ransom, Cliff, "Did Climber Have to Cut Off Arm to Save Life?" *National Geographic*, July 24, 2003, https://www.nationalgeographic.com/culture/2003/07/climber-ralston-amputate-arm-utah/ Accessed on April 16, 2019.

Seligman, Lara, "Mission Impossible: Inside the Dramatic Cave Rescue of a Thai Soccer Team," *Foreign Policy*, September 20, 2018, https://foreignpolicy.com/2018/09/20/mission-impossible-inside-the-dramatic-cave-rescue-of-a-thai-soccer-team/ Accessed on April 16, 2019.

Viswanathan, Radhika, "'This is Madness': A Rescue Diver on What It Was Like to Save the Thai Boys in the Cave," *Vox*, July 12, 2018, https://www.vox.com/2018/7/12/17564360/thai-cave-rescue-boys-mission-diver-ben-reymenants Accessed on April 16, 2019.

INDEX

airplanes, 50–52, 55, 59
Alaska, 28, 30
amputations, 11, 12–14, 48, 55
Arctic Ocean, 28

Blackjack, Ada, 5, 28–37

canyons, 4, 6–8, 10, 13
caverns, 8, 11–12, 14
caves, 4, 16, 18–21, 24–27
cell phones, 8, 14, 19
Chanthawong, Ekkaphon, 17, 19, 22, 27
Colorado, 6–7

depression, 15, 38–39
deserts, 4, 6, 8, 10, 12
divers, 20–23, 25–27

fourteeners, 7, 15

Hall, Rob, 40, 43, 45, 47
hallucinations, 11, 45, 56
hypothermia, 45–46

Inupiat, 30, 35

jungles. See rain forests.

Knight, E. Lorne, 30, 32–34
Koepcke, Juliane, 5, 50–59
Krakauer, Jon, 40, 45
Kunan, Saman, 25

meditation, 17, 22
mountains, 4, 6–7, 16, 18–20, 27, 38–41, 44–46
Mount Everest, 40, 47

national parks, 4

oxygen, 19, 25, 27, 41–44, 46

Peru, 50, 52–53
piranhas, 55
polar bears, 28, 32, 34–37

rain forests, 5, 20, 50, 52–55
Ralston, Aron, 4, 6–8, 10–15
Reymenants, Ben, 22–23
Royal Thai Navy SEALs, 19, 25–26

scurvy, 33
Sherpas, 40, 42–44
Stanton, Richard, 23
Stefansson, Vilhjalmur, 30, 32, 37
supplies, 5–6, 22, 28, 30, 32–33

Thailand, 16, 26
tuberculosis, 37

Utah, 7–8, 15

Volanthen, John, 23–24

water, 4, 6, 10, 14, 16–20, 22, 27, 37, 41, 54–56
Weathers, Beck, 38–46
Wild Boars soccer team, 4, 16–27
Wrangel Island, 28–37

ABOUT THE AUTHOR

Eric Braun is the author of dozens of books for kids and teens on many topics including sports, the deep state, overcoming mistakes, and fractured fairy tales. He lives in Minneapolis with his wife, two sons, and a dog named Willis.